NEW YORK
ISLANDERS

BY LUKE HANLON

Book design by Maggie Villaume
Cover design by Maggie Villaume

Photographs ©: Matt Slocum/AP Images, cover; Frank Franklin II/AP Images, 4–5, 7, 8; Ray Stubblebine/AP Images, 10–11, 13, 15, 19, 23; Richard Drew/AP Images, 16–17, 20; John Dunn/AP Images, 24–25; Kathy Willens/AP Images, 27; Adrian Kraus/AP Images, 29

Press Box Books, an imprint of Press Room Editions.

ISBN
978-1-63494-678-0 (library bound)
978-1-63494-702-2 (paperback)
978-1-63494-748-0 (epub)
978-1-63494-726-8 (hosted ebook)

Library of Congress Control Number: 2022919606

Distributed by North Star Editions, Inc.
2297 Waters Drive
Mendota Heights, MN 55120
www.northstareditions.com

Printed in the United States of America
Mankato, MN
082023

ABOUT THE AUTHOR

Luke Hanlon is a sportswriter and editor based in Minneapolis.

TABLE OF CONTENTS

1

Brock Nelson
tallied 12 points
in 19 games
during the 2021
playoffs.

BROCK AND ROLL

The crowd of 12,000 hopeful fans roared for their New York Islanders. New York led 3–2 in the second round of the 2021 National Hockey League (NHL) playoffs. One more win would clinch the series against the Boston Bruins. The Bruins were a well-tested team. They had played in the Stanley Cup Final just two years prior.

Neither team could grab the momentum in the first period. They went into the intermission tied 1–1. Five minutes into the second, the Islanders' Nick Leddy recovered the puck in his defensive zone. The defenseman's looping pass along the wall found his teammate Josh Bailey. The center lost the puck, but New York's Brock Nelson quickly swooped in and continued the attack. In front of the goal, Nelson made no mistake. He ripped a shot past Bruins goalie Tuukka Rask for a 2–1 Islanders lead.

New York began putting heavy pressure on Boston. Seven minutes later, the Bruins turned the puck over in their own zone. Bailey gathered it and swiftly

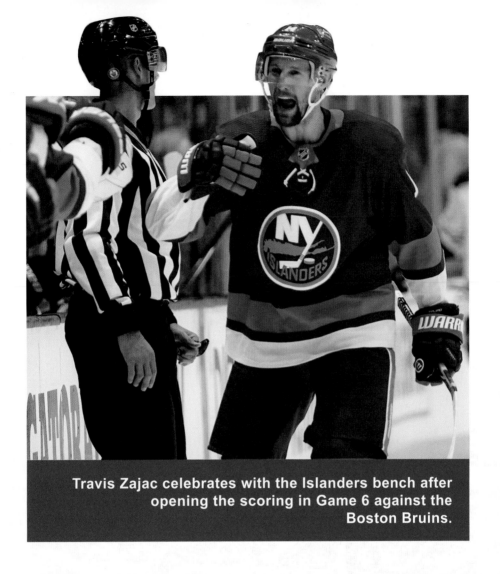

Travis Zajac celebrates with the Islanders bench after opening the scoring in Game 6 against the Boston Bruins.

slid a pass right in front of Rask's goal. Nelson was waiting. His backhand shot tucked between the goalie's legs. Just like that, the Islanders were up 3–1. And they weren't done yet.

Brock Nelson (second from right) celebrates with his teammates after scoring his second goal of Game 6 against the Bruins.

The usually tight Boston defense was flustered. The Bruins lost the puck in front of their goal. This time, it was New York's Kyle Palmieri who made the play. The winger got the puck and stuffed it past Rask to put the Islanders up 4–1.

Boston was playing to keep its season alive. With their dominant second period, the Islanders took control of the game. And their lead only increased in the third period. They cruised to a stunning 6–2 victory. New York was one series shy of the Stanley Cup Final.

• FAREWELL, COLISEUM

The Islanders began playing at Nassau Coliseum on Long Island in 1972. Though it was one of the NHL's smaller arenas, fans embraced it. The Islanders won four Stanley Cups there. After playing some or all of five seasons in Brooklyn, New York, the Islanders played one final season in 2020–21 at Nassau Coliseum. Winger Anthony Beauvillier provided one last memorable moment. He scored the overtime winner in Game 6 of the team's third-round playoff series against the Tampa Bay Lightning. The 3–2 win was the last game ever played in the arena. The Islanders moved into the new UBS Arena the next season.

2

John Tonelli celebrates a teammate's goal against the New York Rangers in a 1979 playoff game.

OUT ON AN
ISLAND

The NHL grew quickly in the late 1960s. The league doubled from 6 to 12 teams in 1967. Two more teams were added in 1970. Then the league added two more teams in 1972, including the New York Islanders. They would play at the newly built Nassau Coliseum on Long Island. That meant they were close, but not too close, to New York's other NHL team, the Rangers.

The first step toward building a team was the expansion draft. The Islanders and Atlanta Flames got to select players from other teams' rosters. The first four picks were all goalies. The Islanders took Gerry Desjardins second overall. Their next selection was Billy Smith. He would go on to play 17 seasons in New York.

However, the Islanders' first season didn't go well. They lost 60 games. At the time, that was an NHL record. But the team made two big additions after the 1972–73 season. New York selected well-rounded defenseman Denis Potvin with the first pick in the 1973 NHL Draft. The Islanders also brought in Al Arbour to be the coach.

Billy Smith (right) didn't begin as the starting goalie in 1972–73. But he went on to have a Hall of Fame career with the Islanders.

Potvin made an impact right away. The Islanders gave up 100 fewer goals in 1973–74 than in the season before.

Potvin also led the team with 54 points. His play earned him the Calder Memorial Trophy. That is given to the best rookie in the NHL each season.

Arbour had only three years of coaching experience. But he had won the Stanley Cup four times as a player. He soon brought his winning ways to Long Island. New York improved by 26 points in 1973–74. Then it improved by another 32 points in 1974–75. That was

•CONSOLATION PRIZE

Not much went right for the Islanders in their first season. But they did get one big win to celebrate. On January 18, 1973, the Islanders played the defending Stanley Cup champion Boston Bruins. The Islanders won 9–7. And 14 of the 16 Islanders skaters who played had either a goal or an assist.

Denis Potvin led the Islanders in points four seasons in a row, starting with his rookie season.

enough to make the playoffs for the

first time.

3

Mike Bossy was an unstoppable goal scorer. He scored a team-record 573 goals in his 10 seasons with New York.

FOUR FOR
FOUR

The Islanders made a run to the semifinals in the 1975 playoffs. But they lost to the Philadelphia Flyers in seven games. The Flyers would go on to win the Cup for the second consecutive year in 1975.

Another big addition helped New York improve further in 1975–76. Center Bryan Trottier recorded 95 points as a 19-year-old rookie. This earned Trottier his own Calder Memorial Trophy. Trottier, alongside defenseman Denis Potvin and goalie Billy Smith, kept the Islanders competitive in the coming years. Two talented wingers helped them take the next step.

Rugged left wing Clark Gillies developed into an All-Star by his third season, in 1976–77. The next year, high-scoring right wing Mike Bossy arrived and won the Calder Trophy. By 1979–80, the "Trio Grande" line of Gillies, Trottier, and Bossy was an offensive force. But the talent didn't end with them. The Islanders were deep across all positions. Their depth allowed coaches to spread ice time more evenly, which kept the players fresh.

Bob Nystrom leaps into the air after scoring the winning goal in the 1980 Stanley Cup Final.

New York reached its first Stanley Cup Final in 1980. Facing the Flyers, the Islanders' Bob Nystrom scored in overtime of Game 6 to secure the Cup at home in Nassau Coliseum. It was only the beginning.

New York got back to the Cup Final in 1981 with ease. And after losing just three

Bryan Trottier led the NHL with 29 points during the 1980 playoffs.

games all postseason, the Islanders beat the Minnesota North Stars in five games to claim another Stanley Cup.

Things only got sweeter in 1981–82. Bossy tallied 147 points. Only two players had ever recorded higher-scoring seasons at the time. No team came close to the Islanders' 54 wins. Reaching their third Final in three years, they swept the

Vancouver Canucks. In 1983, they reached the Final again, this time defeating the Edmonton Oilers in another sweep. The Islanders were at the top of the hockey world.

New York made it back to the Cup Final in 1984. However, this time the Islanders fell to the Oilers in five games. That ended an NHL record of 19 straight playoff series wins for the Islanders.

• SUPER STREAKS

The Islanders are one of two NHL teams to win four Stanley Cups in a row. The other is the Montreal Canadiens. Montreal won four straight from 1976 to 1979. The Canadiens also won five straight from 1956 to 1960. Since the Islanders' run ended, no NHL team has won more than two Stanley Cups in a row.

DENIS POTVIN

Denis Potvin was compared to Boston Bruins great Bobby Orr from a young age. Those were big skates to fill. Many considered Orr to be the best defenseman in NHL history.

Potvin lived up to the expectations. A strong player on both ends of the ice, he won his first Norris Trophy in 1975–76. That trophy is given to the NHL's best defenseman. Potvin ended Orr's eight-year streak of winning the Norris. Potvin won the trophy two more times in his career.

In 1986, Potvin scored his 271st goal. That moved him past Orr for the most goals by a defenseman in NHL history. Potvin ended his career with 1,052 points in 1,060 games.

Al Arbour made Potvin the Islanders' captain in 1979–80. He captained New York to four Stanley Cups. And he spent all 15 seasons of his Hall of Fame career with the Islanders.

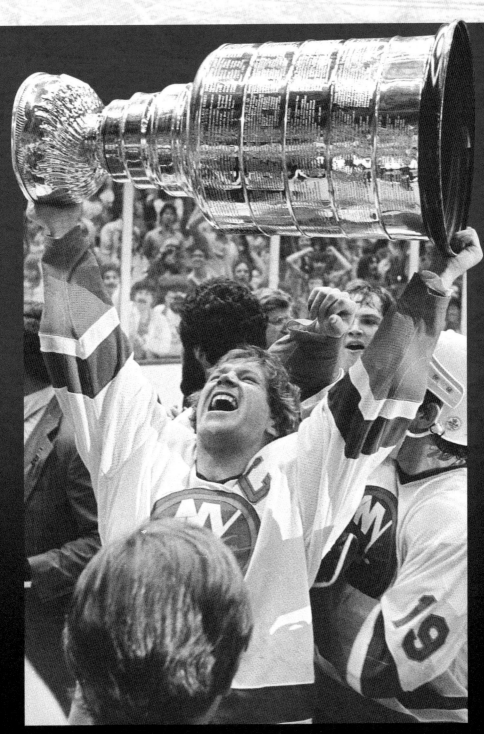

Denis Potvin holds the Stanley Cup over his head after winning it for the second year in a row in 1981.

4

Todd Bertuzzi
skates by a
defender in a
1997 game.

STILL ON THE ISLAND

The Islanders stayed competitive after their Cup runs. But Al Arbour surprised New York when he retired from coaching after the 1985–86 season. He stayed with the team as part of its front office. Then, Mike Bossy retired after the 1986–87 season. During his time in New York, he scored 50 or more goals for nine straight seasons. No other NHL player had accomplished that feat. However, back injuries cut his career short.

The Islanders went on an eight-game losing streak in 1988–89. So the team decided to hire Arbour back as the coach. But the Islanders missed the playoffs. Arbour coached five more seasons before he retired again in 1994.

The Islanders struggled after Arbour stopped coaching. They went

•THE EASTER EPIC

On the evening of April 18, 1987, the Islanders and Washington Capitals faced off in Game 7 of the first round of NHL playoffs. With the score tied 2–2 after regulation, the game headed to overtime. Those extra periods just kept coming. The Islanders eventually scored in the fourth overtime period, winning 3–2. And the game went on so long, it finished in the early hours of April 19, Easter Sunday.

John Tavares (91) wildly celebrates scoring the double-overtime winner in Game 5 with teammate Thomas Hickey (14).

23 years without winning a playoff series. That finally changed in 2016. New York faced the Florida Panthers in the first round. The Islanders won Game 5 in double overtime to take a 3–2 series lead. Islanders captain John Tavares created more drama in Game 6. He scored to tie the game 1–1 in the final minute of the

third period. The star center then scored the overtime winner on a wraparound shot to clinch a series win.

Two years later, Tavares left the team as a free agent. He had been with the Islanders since 2009. In seven of his nine seasons with the Islanders, he was the team's leading scorer.

The Islanders surprised many by reaching the playoffs in 2018–19. Young center Mathew Barzal took over as the main scorer. Fellow center Brock Nelson emerged as another reliable scorer. Hardworking wing Anders Lee led the team as captain. And in 2020 and 2021, the Islanders were just one series win shy of the Stanley Cup Final.

Mathew Barzal (13) won the Calder Trophy in 2017–18 after recording a team-high 85 points.

A three-year playoff streak came to an end in 2021–22. There was still reason to celebrate, though. With a new arena and talented players such as Barzal, Lee, and Nelson, fans had hope that more playoff memories were coming soon.

NEW YORK ISLANDERS
QUICK STATS

TEAM HISTORY: New York Islanders (1972–)

STANLEY CUP CHAMPIONSHIPS: 4 (1980, 1981, 1982, 1983)

KEY COACHES:

- Al Arbour (1973–86, 1988–94, 2007): 740 wins, 537 losses, 223 ties

- Jack Capuano (2010–17): 227 wins, 192 losses, 64 overtime losses

- Barry Trotz (2018–22): 152 wins, 102 losses, 34 overtime losses

HOME ARENA: UBS Arena (Elmont, NY)

MOST CAREER POINTS: Bryan Trottier (1,353)

MOST CAREER GOALS: Mike Bossy (573)

MOST CAREER ASSISTS: Bryan Trottier (853)

MOST CAREER SHUTOUTS: Glenn "Chico" Resch (25)

Stats are accurate through the 2021–22 season.

GLOSSARY

CAPTAIN
A player who serves as the leader of a team.

DRAFT
An event that allows teams to choose new players coming into a league.

EXPANSION
The way leagues grow by adding new teams.

FRONT OFFICE
The workers who manage the business side of a sports team.

ROOKIE
A first-year player.

WRAPAROUND
When a player starts on one side of the net, skates behind the net, and shoots on the other side.

ZONE
One of three areas on a hockey rink that are separated by blue lines.

TO LEARN MORE

BOOKS

Davidson, B. Keith. *NHL*. New York: Crabtree Publishing, 2022.

Doeden, Matt. *G.O.A.T. Hockey Teams*. Minneapolis: Lerner Publications, 2021.

Duling, Kaitlyn. *Women in Hockey*. Lake Elmo, MN: Focus Readers, 2020.

MORE INFORMATION

To learn more about the New York Islanders, go to **pressboxbooks.com/AllAccess.**

These links are routinely monitored and updated to provide the most current information available.

INDEX